ON ~~UN~~BECOMING

AESTHETIC EVOLUTION OF THIS RISING ANCESTOR

A Poetic Memoir by Hokis

Hokis

hokis publishing | remote location

ON~~UN~~BECOMING: Aesthetic Evolution of This Rising Ancestor

First published in 2020 by Hokis - USA
www.hokis.blog
ISBN: 9798691161872

Author photo by Rosen-Jones Photography

Editorial support: Kelly Garriot Waite, Haley Heidemann, Tianna G. Hansen, Tracy Blake, and Nadia Gerassimenko

Design and layout assistance: Tim Paxton, Will Blake, Stuart M. Buck, and Jeremy Gaulke.

Copyright © 2020 Hokis. All rights reserved. No part of this publication may be reproduced, stored in or introduced into a retrieval system, or transmitted in any form, or by any means (electronic, mechanical, photocopying, recording or otherwise) without prior written permission of the publisher. Any person who does any unauthorized act in relation to the publication may be liable for criminal prosecution and civil claims for damages.

Dedications

∞

This is dedicated to
Dr. Christine Blasey Ford,
the parents who Life-d me,
the partner who turned towards me,
the gaslighter who mirrored me,
the womxn who held my stories,
and my Soldier Hip's consistent reminder:

Reality is what you choose it to be.

∞

ON~~UN~~BECOMING: Aesthetic Evolution of This Rising Ancestor

CONTENT NOTE

∞

Here lies the collection's most challenging piece to write - the content note. I prefer not to use "content warning," as it turns on sirens and flashing lights right from the get-go. I am not down playing the storyline here. I recognize to be a survivor of anything, you first must have at least one unthinkable thing happen to you. This poetic memoir includes a few unthinkable things - appropriately described, with well-placed curse words, vengeful vignettes, and metamorphosis-like imagery. My hope is that each page moves you through the vulnerable process of self-forgiveness.

So instead of flicking on your limbic system with a warning, I invite you to consider this a call-to-courage story. The main character is a grief-stricken Womxn who accepts Life's invitation to the dark corners of her mind to heal from a traumatic past - which includes a sexual assault.

I believe empowerment is a self-timed process and cannot be forced. A large part of rising above your past is to trust your sense of things. Perhaps this book calls you in, perhaps your body doesn't offer its consent. There is no "should" with healing, there is only trust. No matter if you purchase this book or put it back on the shelf, I support you and wish you well.

ONUNBECOMING: Aesthetic Evolution of This Rising Ancestor

TABLE OF CONTENTS
∞

- 7 Prologue: THICKER THAN BLOOD
- 11 FORE the love of WORDs by *The Ancestors*
- 15 preFACE: in with THE EXhale

Chapter 1: THE PRESENT, A GIFT
- 24 CODE DEPENDENT's Glare
- 26 Firestorm Winds
- 29 The Hike of Taking a Hike
- 31 Drips of Dew

Chapter 2: ENTERS: This Martyr's Therapist
- 34 Suicide Notes May Vary
- 35 Night Sky
- 36 tickling ITs catastrophe
- 39 Lopsided Truth
- 41 Dark Light of Day
- 42 HERE, just take (fuck) IT
- 43 Freed

Chapter 3: THE SURGEON GENERAL'S WARNING
- 46 Epigenetic Reverb
- 47 I Am [not a] Substance
- 48 Truth's's a[d]Version
- 49 Confession of a Former Cult Leader
- 50 Dominatrix Rattler

Chapter 4: CODE SWITCHING
- 53 Because
- 55 Geneva Conventions
- 57 Pistols, Stamens, and Spikes
- 59 Silent Breakfast to Go

Chapter 5: rIcochet
- 62 Uncaring Dangers
- 63 Hovering Fruitchild
- 64 Abled-Body Partner
- 65 [Yet Untitled]
- 66 Sapling's Apology

Chapter 6: gratitUde
- 70 Vertebrae Rising
- 71 Over, Around, Under, and Through
- 73 Daft Light
- 75 It's Poetic Justice Until We All Lose Our Eyes
- 76 Faithing With My Tidal Powers
- 78 Return to the Crooked Willow

Chapter 7: exHAIL WITH the IN
- 82 Good, Then Extra
- 84 Malignant Phraseology Vol. 1: "You're the Crazy One"
- 86 Familiar, Familial Border
- 88 plated projectIon
- 90 waking in the center of the Dark Triad

Chapter 8: AFTER THANKS is GIVEN
- 94 [s]Pacing of Constants
- 95 Altering the Mind of Gravity
- 96 Preference Over Judgement
- 99 Synapse Surfing
- 101 Sleeping Beauty

Chapter 9: ACHEKNOWLEDGEments
- 106 Ancestral Rise
- 108 Arrow Through That Universal Moon
- 110 Leader of the Free World

- 112 In Summary
- 116 Glossary

ON~~UN~~BECOMING: Aesthetic Evolution of This Rising Ancestor

Prologue: THICKER THAN BLOOD

∞

At the age of 22, I met the 63-year-old Armenian woman who had given me up for adoption. On the evening of that breathtaking day I stood in her bedroom. We spoke through our reflection in the mirror in front of us. I felt small, not in the five-foot way I was used to, but in the little girl-in-awe-of-her-elder way. She spoke brilliantly of Yerevan, of roasted lamb, and the importance of skilled tailors – all the while disrobing in front of me. For the first time my inner child was able to gaze upon the future of its olive-hued shape.

This was not the tall, slim body of the European woman who'd raised me. This was a thick-hipped, unapologetic, Middle-Eastern woman. Her skin was freckled with moles, like the moonlit sky I would often look up to when my restless soul couldn't sleep. I wondered if her heart might also be reaching towards that universal moon and, perhaps, thinking of me. Until this privileged moment, I hadn't realized just how deeply I longed for this quantum entanglement.

Mother told me stories of the Armenian genocide and of *our Mount Ararat*. After minutes passed, she paused with intent, as to say "Pay attention now, my child." Her spine was straight, fully embodying her matronly figure, suited-up with a thick strapped brassiere and delicate hosiery. It was then she told me that our ancestors leapt from Mount Ararat to save themselves from rape and murder; to save their children from Earthly suffering.

This drawn-out jolt caused my world to spin. I felt drunk and dizzy from skin and truth. "Skin, truth, and leaping to save oneself. Common themes of this survivor," I thought. I stood convinced she'd been looking over me through that universal moon. Why else would this be the first family story she shared? Even a generation and 22 years apart, we both understood patterns of victimization are more than skin deep.

She has since passed, resting in the galaxy with our universal moon. Still, our bloods' knowing is with me; it continues to save me in those moments when I cannot seem to save myself.

ON~~UN~~BECOMING: Aesthetic Evolution of This Rising Ancestor

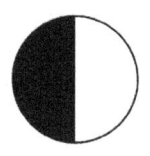

FORE the love of WORDs
by The Ancestors

∞

*{Father Time passed –
easing Her noisy memories of stifling days.
She is now free to lay down, blanketed by silence
and the finite Light of the firefly.}*

The Passing Of Father, Time

"If I close my eyes, and
turn my head,
will time go away?"

                                        {You will.
                                        Time will be with her now,
                                        She will tend to all you leave

                                        Life no longer,
                                        yet with Time,
                                        continues to flow

                                        in the truth of Her brow and
                                        the ink of Her pen. After
                                        all, her Life is a promise made.

                                        rest peacefully knowing, she will.}

"NEVER FORGET –
we do not make promises
we cannot keep."

Vulgata

{puzzle, puzzle
go away
come again another day.

breath
stare there, at the
table, at the

last piece
left, it is all on her.

as waiting turns to covet,
she must say goodbye to infantile-
inoculated crimes.

no more fetal
position, She is
born;
Her life.
Your life.
the infinity of Life.

It is not up to His's words.
It is not vulga\r\ta.
It is her right-to-life.
It is her t\HYMN\e.}

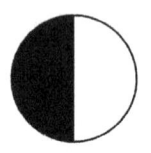

ON~~UN~~BECOMING: Aesthetic Evolution of This Rising Ancestor

preFACE: in with THE EX hale

∞

Grieving the normalcy that made yesterday true,
knowing tomorrow won't be better, and
nobody believes
 sees it like
 you.

Daggers on Ice
Penned in a dream with Dr. Christine Blasey Ford (September 26, 2018)

Pour me another glass of words.
I feel the need to punch your face.
I opened this as the winds called me.

Now we muddle
in the scum of my wake.

I'm afraid I've done it again, you see.
I've placed the dagger meant for you,
cleanly into me.

Brown Room in the White House

Part I
In the House around the corner.

"I just want to know what it feels like,"

he said to me, my pants pulled down and arms held above my head. (labor day before junior year)

The large cork board to the left.
    A poster of Kiss, in full makeup (disguise),
    Spinal Tap (the mockumentary),
    Farrah in her red bathing suit (buffet of descriptors).

The bed was filled with water.

The walls were brown.

My right hip froze in fear –
    decades later, this Soldier Hip grips when I grieve.

"I just want to know what it feels like"

Those words, all alone, sitting in my memory.
 Just. Those. Words.
    "I just want (to invade you so I can learn)"
    "I just want (you to give in so I can feel what I want)."
    "I just want (you to sit here quietly and do what I say)."
    "I just want (you to go along with the lie that this is right)."
    "I just want (you to realize your place in the world)."
    "I just want (you to lay there, silent, and wait for me to learn)."

There. That's it.
"Wait, I need to pretend you aren't here, so I can   ."

Part II

I was four when my cat was attacked by the neighbor's dog - thrown around like a chew toy in my front yard. I ran into the house for my parents' help – loud, panicked, and without concern for life on the inside.

"Shhhhhhh, this is important. We are watching this. Wait."

It was 1974. The news of Tricky Dick's House.

The news. Politics.
The noise of politics takes up space,
                                        my space.

I froze.

I waited.

When my spacetime came. It was too late.

That night, my cat sat in the disposal side of the sterile, stainless steel sink. Panting. In pain. Dying. No vet. No pain killer. No mercy killing. I sat in the sinkhole next to her, to comfort us.

    Waiting for her to no longer suffer.
    Knowing suffering comes and goes -
    all we can do is be with.
    The waiting to be heard.
    The waiting for the death.

    Death, the consequence of waiting.

    It changed me inside
                           my four-year-old self.

I was uninterested in Tricky Dick,
I was the one in the second sinkhole.
I was the one comforting.

My role was decided – to wait, let them learn, and comfort.
I've become the master of waiting.

My Soldier Hip tells me when I wait too long, whispers –
> *Some people will take advantage of your waiting.*
> *Sometimes waiting is beautiful.*
> *Sometimes waiting is compassionate.*
> *Sometimes waiting is a slow fuck.*
> *Sometimes waiting is rape.*
> *Sometimes waiting is death.*

Funny, the ways life teaches us to discern subtle meanings.
I don't want to learn this,
and I don't want to wait.

Part III
2017
Trump's House.
> Where tricks are turned for dicks and
> souls for phallacies
#Metoo.
> Permission granted – forced.
> (BROWN ROOM. BROWN ROOM.)
> {*remember. remember.*}

1974
Nixon is the decade's distraction.
The abstraction of the world's ailings, dosed down to
the TVspoon we can swallow and still keep down.
Gets us just angry enough, but not angry enough.
It happens in that little box we can turn off.
In that other neighborhood.
In that other house.
In that other person.

Nixon distracted people.
Nixon killed my cat.

Nixon raped me.
2018
24-hour news
Pocket-sized TVspoons
"Likes" and "Friends"
Trump - the decade's distraction.
        The resulting cognitive dissonance
                silences alter boys
                and children in cages

        "Be quiet and wait." They say.

        "What happens in the meantime?" I reply.

        My ears turn toward the sounds inside
                              my house.
                              (me).

Part IV
2018
In my house.
They move toward the attention they seek.
Familiar way of connecting or,
perhaps, familiar ache for connection.

        Mocumentaries.
        Political satire.
        Women in bathing suits.
        Alter boys.
        TVspoon sized playgrounds.
        Fallacies.
        Rightness Anger.
        Truth in politics.
        Truth from death.

        (Truth, I do the same.)

In my house,
        I ache for marathon ears.
        I ache for exposed eyes.
        I ache for vouchsafe hands.
        For not waiting until death do us part.

I don't seek reporting.
        new[s] fallacies
        and the hushing of trickster dicks

I seek to share stories;
        Me stories.
        You stories.
        We stories.

In my house
        I will no longer wait.
        I listen and speak from my Soldier Hip
                              (in my inside's
                                    outside voice).

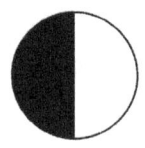

ON~~UN~~BECOMING: Aesthetic Evolution of This Rising Ancestor

ON~~UN~~BECOMING: Aesthetic Evolution of This Rising Ancestor

Chapter 1: THE PRESENT, A GIFT

∞

Panic shines in the dark –
where the external moon rises
and the internal sun won't set.
The longer we placate this purgatory,
we pointlessly pay for their debts.

CODE DEPENDENT's glare

And then
There is the day when they truly need you.
When he loses his legs,
And her denial-powered anger commands
He win his body's war with gravity.

And then
There is the week when they truly need you.
When he cannot find himself,
And the wildflower prairie fills with weeded dendrites -
A field that has taken too many comrades.

And then
There is the year they truly need you.
When he is networking his own synthetic cables
throughout the world-wide-web,
And you are the tuning fork -
Affirming the self that was here before he remembered who he will be.

She stares there, at the tarnished heirloom locket's engraving:
>On these days
>Before they truly needed you
>You needed them to need you.
>
>You needed them to entangle
>Their need for you, with the want of you -
>Enabling them to stay.
>
>You weaved the perfect nest with translucent spider silk.
>A nest they w\c\ould never leave,
>Like the quick, polished petite hummingbird that you are.

And now
They no longer care to fit.

> Your wings' frantic exhaustion has taken you from view.
> You lose not your legs, rather your footing.
> Your chained dendrites are entangled with your own weeds,
> cables, and recycled spider silk.

And now
You are the only one who needs you.

Firestorm Winds

Kiss me like you are grateful for me. That

I exist.

Not because

I am

special, but because my flesh and blood are alive,
now, on this planet.
Because I chose you to heal me.
Because I trust\ed you to embrace that honor,
and you promised you would.

Kiss me like you want me,
not want to want me
not to prove you are worthy of love
not to avoid loneliness
not to feel you've won me in the secret war men have over
the territory of Cunt.

Kiss me with cellular knowledge that

I am

the only combination of the lonely bones
entwined in a moving heap.
Frozen in spacetime.
In an apartment, in the Paris of the Middle East.

An address now occupied by the flag of ISIS,
    joyfear and
        gun-shaped fallacies.

Kiss me in a way that honors the struggle of
the international incident that

I am.

Kiss me in a way that makes up for all the
    angst,
    guilt, and
    secrets
    my existence spawned.

Kiss me like you are grateful
for the spark
for the infidelity that

I am.

Kiss me remembering I was once a child,
conceived around the corner from the now refugee-quarter.
We children need to play
                be taken from the Truth of their species.
                    kick the can.
                    hide and seek.
                    dress-up.
                  , to overtly and intensely, pretend.

Kiss me as if there is no end,
No climax,
No satisfaction.
Kiss me because
there is now, and that is everything – and enough.

Kiss me remembering
The luscious switch that turns off the noise.
        (Do you hear the noise?
                believe in the switch?
                need it as I do?)

Kiss me as an act of rebellion
our breath – the firestorm winds
can reach the wounds of my ancestors, reignite
my land with Purpose.

No power to own.
No power to win.
No personified missiles.
No flags in territories.
No covert operations.
No pushing and pulling against gravity.
No thrusting forward like a marathon runner.
No winning the race, only to leave orphans behind.

Sometimes my story is just my story,
my decades of walking.
Then I wake to remember my DNA dances with the story
of distant me's,
   you's,
   us's,
   them's.

Swaying in rhythm with each and every act that did, or
did not, happen.

I need you to help me forget this burden, or
        {she worries}
        in my orphaned scurry
        to make it all go away,
        I may very well forget you, in order to survive.
            This is what orphans do.
            This is what survivors do.
            This, then, is what I do.
            {she wonders}

This is not my wish,
yet it's not up to me.
Nature pushes me to thrive.
                        The firestorm winds are calling me.

The Hike of Taking a Hike

Part I
What I mean:

You didn't open me.
The wind did.
So stay away from the crumbs
that fall from my pack
as I scurry down the road.

They are meant for the helpless animals.

Maybe I will see you at the end of the trail of "Courage".

It would be a tragedy if you didn't make it -
Yet, y\our life is y\our own.

Part II
What I say:

Don't mind me.
I am just looking for myself.

Here under this heavy boulder, or
I might be burrowing into earth with the bugs.
       up in the night sky.
          shining brightly with like-minded twinkles.
          remembering in the embrace of an old friend.

The winds tell me to look in the arena, for
I have never been meant for the stands.

Don't take it personally, but take it and run.
I cannot promise protection.
(I am exhausted.)

I have always been told to put myself first.
The loneliness I feared is now realized.
I am handicapped by amnesia –
Who is this "self" I am to put first?
Where do I find her?

The winds say she is there –
In the dirt digging,
the star gazing, and
the holding of age-old friends.

I cannot love anyone else right now,
This pocketbook of change carries equity for one.
I hope you find relief, no longer required to figure me out –
the frightening puzzle to reciprocate love with.

The hardest part of looking for myself is knowing
you may not feel hopeful or relieved.

I hate this
yet not as much as
I hate that
we each have lost
our inside maps.

Drips of Dew

Long ago and far away,
atop a mountain,
Promises were made.

Ideal, naive selves present.
Words without witness
fall too easily
to the ground.

Do they splash or pop?
Or land with great thud?
No.
The words slowly drip, like
morning dew sinks
into the forever forest floor.

One day woken, the forest overgrown.
Not with the words that planted it,
but the lost intentions
of past pain sounds.

Hold my hand,
but let me be.
None of this is fair.

Hold my hand,
and walk away.
Breathe in the crisp fresh air.

ON~~UN~~BECOMING: Aesthetic Evolution of This Rising Ancestor

Chapter 2: ENTERS: This Martyr's Therapist

∞

Our stories hide
between couch cushions and
empty medicine vials –
that first read, so sweet.

Suicide Notes May Vary

Torch Bearer!
{Gaslighter?}

Shine your dusk
through these cracks of
Me, too.

I willingly welcome your dirty, burning
diesel-fueled torch
into my home.

With your carefully curated notes
your symphonic form of
{orchestrated} courtship swoon,

please

make this
once again
orphaned self's half-baked
cult mind up for me.

Set your versions-of-me free.

Night Sky

Yesterday's dark night rests
in contrast to this starlit sky, watch your
chirp powered clouds;
   move,
   disperse,
   take new shape,
       leave.

The ever-present distant plane;
   freckled,
   blue,
   milky.
       detach.

The playful clouds.
   The warm hand.
   You see,
   I see,
   we see.
       fall.

Then they're gone;
   the cartoon duck,
   the turtle sticking out her tongue,
   the dragons.
       (Soldier Hip asks, "Why did he see so many dragons?")

tickling ITs catastrophe

"*Can I stop by?*
I need to sew on a button.

Can I stop by?
I need your advice.

Can I stop by?
I am shaking.
I don't like you seeing me like this.
I appreciate you.

I have cancer.
I drink too much.

I want to get clean.
I want to join the navy.

I am thankful for the bed to rest.
Let's walk. Let's talk.
Do you *want to read my favorite poetry book?*
This song is **for you.**

I can do that myself!
I am a master chef, you know.

I can get him a job to support his habit.
I've got a blunt for him
{smirk as testing}

I wanted to see what you would do.
I laugh when I'm scared.
It won't happen again.

You *ruined my special day, do you see that?*

I fix everything with ketchup and **blame you** *for its taste.*

You're overthinking this.

*I'm going to be with someone
who wants to be with* **me***.*

*Asian women are tight.
Black women are strong.
White women are white bread in bed.
Why is this weird to talk about?*

There is no room for **me** *to be myself here.
I have to find a less worse place than this.*

You are dead to **me***.*

*Can I stay three more days?
Both the girls are staying the night.
Acid drop Monday times three.
This is the best day.
I wouldn't have it any other way.*

You're important to **me***.*
You could *be my baby.*
You can *call me daddy.*

*He broke my arm when I was five,
This is why I stay numb.*
You gotta *stop letting them take you for granted.*

*I have nowhere to go,
Can I come over for Thanksgiving?*

*I will judge you for being stupid.
That shirt looks nice* **on you***.
He deserves to be punched in the face.*

ONUNBECOMING: Aesthetic Evolution of This Rising Ancestor

Are mad at me for saying that?
I'm using again, **see my tracks**.

Those shoes are the worst.
Let's go for a walk in the woods.
Let's toss rocks in the pond and forget.

My *friend died,*
Can you *come?*

I am going to sue my boss for spying on me,
Can you *help me?*

I don't think you fully grasp what I'm saying;
I'm leaving this earth,
Will **you come** *say good-bye?*

Never mind,
She asked **me** *to marry her.*

She is good for **me**.
She is a painter,
But it is nothing like your poetry.

I don't hide who I am.
I will never leave.
{smirk with threat}

I am your pit.
{smirk as entitlement}

I want *to show you something.*
I think you'd like it.
It's called knife play.
{smirk is contempt}

*

You don't know me.

38

Lopsided Truth

truth
shifts to trust
with one required
base pair reassignment.

trutH;
drop the grand Hoax
shush the lies to self and others
sink back into your primordial slime
reorganize, safely within your self-made cocoon.

trust;
        Subtype 1 - truSt;
        add the ultimate Sacrifice
        to give up who you are
        emerge with naked wings exposed
        trusting self to know, who is/is not that kind of hungry.

        Subtype 2- truST;
        seekers are not made for 'us'
        they pine for Self-Trust
        have a little extra need
        a different species entirely.

        Subtype 3 - truF;
        beware, with this species
        there comes a risky mutation.
        replaces a base pair, ST
        with a cocky single, F.
                I wonder if
                a single nucleotide for the price of a base pair
                is a good-for-evolution
                kind of trade,

ON~~UN~~BECOMING: Aesthetic Evolution of This Rising Ancestor

I guess I will ask
the lopsided
butterfly.
oh look,
        it flew away.

      wait,
            it was never here.

            F, is for Fictional.
            Fictional truF.

            Keep your eye out
            for this lopsided breed.

Dark Light of Day

In the inevitable Light that rises
from deciding dark's end,
my mortality mistook silence for lack of noise.

Woken by the sky dragon's fire,
my Soldier Hip prepares.

The remains of me retreat,
soul and skin recall
this well-rehearsed play.

Pen inked with Her immortal Light,
readied for the patiently waiting
moral of Her story's
moonrise.

ON~~UN~~BECOMING: Aesthetic Evolution of This Rising Ancestor

fuck
HERE, just ~~take~~ IT

He/She/Them
It's the same dance.
Two people. Two experiences of the same story.
No wide-angle lens.

I am humming, buzzing, kissing with soulhands.
They are along for the ride,
whatever ride that makes their shoulders shrug,
whatever crumb of pleasure they can squander
for their frightened heart,
and always thinking the other hes/shes/Theys have it wrong.

Maybe they hear some questions to answer along the way;
maybe they choose to wonder.
Mostly they don't until they fear.

Inside my house.
Am I choosing to wonder?
Or is it true what they say, my sister-daughters and brother-sons?
I do not choose, rather I have been chosen.
The spirits have placed me in this dimension of mine.
The solo player in the high-stakes heart game.
The preacher and congregation of
"The Church of FOR FUCKING CHRIST, You Are Enough."

No matter the form, the rules, the structure.
No matter the he/she/them, it is all the same dance.
It is all just the lonely game of words.

They just want to know what it feels like.
I can comply and rape myself, again.

Words. wOrds. woRds. worDs. wordS.
(Well, fuck it. Fuck them. Turn up the noise and just fuck.)

Freed

there is poly as in amorous and
poly as in pimp le

t me pick at that scab
until it falls limp,

leech it

or let
it bleed.

ON~~UN~~BECOMING: Aesthetic Evolution of This Rising Ancestor

ON~~UN~~BECOMING: Aesthetic Evolution of This Rising Ancestor

Chapter 3: SURGEON GENERAL'S WARNING

∞

If you gaslight that cigarette, it
will turn on my self-righteous flame.

Epigenetic Reverb

The strong sun shimmers:
{There will be no genocide today. no martyrs to make.

> *We do not waste time on trifles.*
> *Leap, my daughter, from yourself.*
> *Fly off the edge of tonight's Mount\ed Ararat*
> *if that's what it takes.*
>
> *We do not fret for your fall.*
> *The anchoring foothills of Noah's long journey are soft.*
>
> *We do not recommend you ignore your irredentist*

agitation.

> *You won the war of self-protection over-attachment*
> *One hundred years ago and again, unwittingly,*
> *the day you were born.}*

the waiting Wind weeps:
{species like us understand divinity is no easy feat.}

       *

I am

revis\v\ed by their iridescent whispers.

The now-imprinted
epigenetic reverb serenades,
historical sacrificial-freedom
tuned to self-sufficient flight.

I AM [not a] SUBSTANCE

Of Substance:
        the real physical matter
        a person consists,
        more than exists.
        Together, privacy, bounded truth.
        Tangible, solid presence.
        Important,
        Valid,
        Significant.

A Substance:
        the real physical matter
        a thing consists,
        no one exists.
        Separate, covert, solo act.
        Intangible, alte\a\red truth.
        Vanishing,
        Codependent,
        Significant.

I am not a substance,
there is nothing left to use here.

In my absence, I am substantial.
        What you pine for is
        pretty fucking
        Inconsequential.

In my absence, I am substantial.
        What you pine for,
        pretty fucking,
        is inconsequential.

TRUTH'S a[d]VERSION

To him
Her suicide note reads
Like a concentrated dose
Of all her victim issues
In one syringe –

Little does he know
Her religion prohibits
Needles.

To Truth
His suicide note reads
Like a concentrated dose
Of her redirected rage
In one syringe –

Little does he know
She finds his track marks
Victorious.

Amen

Confessions of a Former Cult Leader

As you rush towards
my hijacked ambulance –
the karambit steady,
resting to the side of my birthing, Soldier Hip.

Your momentum,
not mine,
disembowels you
to expose
the cancer
that never existed
inside the you that you aren't.

It's not your fault:
You weren't privileged with,
though you probably should have asked,
my safe word:

Manson.

Dominatrix Rattler

I listen from the mountaintop
Where ancestors teach; covert, slithering whispers,

{This, my winged-daughter, is an exceptional way to fly.}

I catch my Earthly prey's vibration
With my seem-to-them shuddering
Dominatrix tail.
I whip them and skin them
From toes to sky.

Pausing at the foothills of
Their jugular
Pulsing with rancid nourishment to
The crown of their peak.

The subtle, painless slit
Made under the jaw.
Stiletto holds it steady.
Razor red nails reach inside.
Carving space,
Between dermis and meat.

Gristle meets soulhands,
Snapped with a sudden twist.
No vessel is too sized,
For the unhinged jaw of this mind.

ON~~UN~~BECOMING: Aesthetic Evolution of This Rising Ancestor

ON~~UN~~BECOMING: Aesthetic Evolution of This Rising Ancestor

ONUNBECOMING: Aesthetic Evolution of This Rising Ancestor

Chapter 4: CODE SWITCHING

∞

If I gaslight your cigarette, it
will reverse the supply chain.

Because

I like the feel of dopamine's hand as it leads me to the apple'd tree.
I have a God complex, believing the only person to help is me.

I was told your name one mournful day, long before.
I made a promise to settle a sister's score.

I am angry and want someone to pay.
I saw it would be easy that first day.

I remember her when she was little, and you when she was dead.
I am the secret keeper, and you were her dread.

the obvious solution is a federal crime.
I made a promise to meet her need without doing time.

there is something romantic about running someone out of town.
to spew familiar rhetoric to the self-identified king, who is truly the clown.

as expected, your eyes were on the wrong ball.

I know this,
because I am a woman and this is how men, great or not, always do fall.

Geneva Conventions

{Some are born without a self, you know.}

Have the "you" been gone so long
the lighthouse we offer
signals pain, not safety, to
ITs Light-sensitive,
compartmentalized mind;
    created.
    enabled.
    emboldened.

The triangled-circle gathers,
to water-weave all the fluid truths.
hovering above our vertigo confusion

We see your suffering.
    (An eye you counted on.)
We don't blame you.
    (A perspective you chose us for.)
We then wonder.
    (To rise above, not play along.)

If we are not a lighthouse, but the squeal of an unwanted ambulance –
    What is our role?
    Do we exist?
    Do we matter?
        (Questioning that cums with your brand of play.)

The ambulance turns, with sirens' song
The Water-Weavers work from their individual wisdom.
Empowered by their hivemind.
Illusionists and improvisers.
An expression of exuberant non-attachment.

We clear a path to the lighthouse,
render it to the non-IT-thems.

Who pines for this beacon, we cannot control.
Who follows these crumbs, we cannot decide.

These offerings \if abandoned\
will be the lore of our deathbed regrets.

Pistols, Stamens, and Spikes

"The only way is to hug the cactus."
Her inebriated lips
casually spill over the lap of IT.

"I guess this means you must hug me."
IT speaks.
"With each puncture,
 you will learn to breathe. My intent is not to hurt you.

{I am certain IT seeks to not collapse into breath.}

She hears in ITs stories,
the eye for interconnection.

{I don't trust your sense-is-able.}

The wisdom in her pained-past stories are quieted.
If woken, they could speak
through her artist-hand:
It all matters - even the nothing.
OH! Especially the nothing.
Each structure of nothing, love
keeps the everything cactus alive.
The patterns repeat from core to sky.
Making love.

{Please, only if you feel truly safe.}

Without the hooked central spine,
She would not see inside.
Without the unusual flattened spine,
her soul loving hands would not touch.
Without the varied spine,
she could not be open to needed lessons.

Even the cactus
requires roots.
A single burly taproot.
Tendrilly, independent spine roots.

{Remember to reserve your rare adventitious root for those attuned to your heart's naked love.}

Fucking a cactus,
is a demonstration in the streets.
Soon forgotten, in the noise of the noise.
Loving a cactus,
THAT is a lollapalooza.
Leaving remains,
sticky love-soaked memories.
Propelling us forward.
Pereskia flowers open to the sun.

{Turn towards your doubtful desert-rain's whisper:
"Are the words 'fucking' and 'love' reversed for IT?"*}*

There is more to a desert earth flower,
than the point in which the spike enters her skin.

The structure of nature,
mimics throughout
the everything of the nothing.

This rising ancestor speaks:
{There is no everything, in this form's nothing.}

Silent Breakfast to Go

Whiskey sour.
Whiskey sweet.
Wisk her heart.

Beat her
Eggs into an om
Lette her devour it
From a thirstless hunger.

You know best,
After all.

And yet,
She knows enough
Not to run on
An empty stom
Ache.

...
Stom; soundless, silent.

ON~~UN~~BECOMING: Aesthetic Evolution of This Rising Ancestor

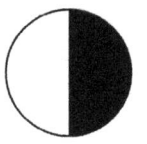

ON~~UN~~BECOMING: Aesthetic Evolution of This Rising Ancestor

Chapter 5: rIcochet

∞

When the gaslit cigarette bursts,
it turns off all rights for blame.

Uncaring Dangers

i miss the me you reminded me i am.
i miss the me hidden
under my lifetime assignment of
crazy-making altruism.

i miss the turnover permitted with
the three-moon-cycled term
allowing me to change with the wind, be indifferent
when it was normal to be reckless and naive.

i miss the me that only listened to music and lectures,
found bodily power-plays in the night.

i miss the me wrapped up in the not IT you.
that me projected onto you, like so many reels before.
i ache for her.

curious,
how in order to find her
i must say good-bye
to all the ITs and yous.

it's my first act of rebellion,
my tantrum, if you will,
that returns old me
to this me.

(Was I ever there?)

the insightful dominos tip and fall into this Self:
When basking in the Light of kindness,
Indifference
        strips altruism of its compulsive pathology.
        is necessary to truly love.
        offers delay from uncaring dangers in the night.
        is authentic loving care.

Hovering Fruitchild

hate and anger
anger and indifference
indifference and love
love and hate
hate and indifference
indifference and indifference
hate and hate
love and love

the fruitchild doesn't hover far from the tree.
the courtship pairing,
informs the innate sixth sense
that exists in between
skylit canopy and
roothidden dirt.

Able-Bodied Partner

Makeup for father's childhood.
Makeup for mother's vexation.
Makeup for eldest's judgement.
Makeup for middle's shame-filled indignation.

I am holding daddy's hands,
while pushing mom to leave.
I float above the first brother's judgement.
I giggle with the second,
until he's bitten by narcissistic fleas.

Who am I in this balancing act,
if not Compensator for unmet needs?
I was the big little sister, well placed as space holder,
learning to see them, skip over me.

The master at sleight of hand black magic,
I prefer straight forward, but can play the game.
Mostly I am just funny, even delightful,
courageously kind, in a loyal frame.

I don't want to be special,
Buffed to shine.
If you want to know the truth,

~~I want a~~
~~I want to be a~~
I am a wolf –
Distinctly attached, instinctively loyal –
An able-bodied partner in crime.

[Yet Untitled]

shhhhhhhhhhhh..........
I'm here now
I will solve your problem
(like it or not)
In fact, I must
My life depends on it.

shhhhhhh........
Your compensation for God's inadequacies is here now
I will take that bullet
(you won't feel a thing)
In fact, I must
My identity depends on it.

shhh.......
my well-rehearsed moment is always available
I shapeshift into any character
(always on the edge of the razor)
In fact, I obsess
On how to quiet my noise of your numbed indecision
My soul fights for it.

shIT!
Your relay teammate has dropped the baton of fate
I can no longer worry about deserting her
(wrists sore, hands free)

The fact is, I dance fiercely, love loudly,
see clearly with my high functioning third eye.
My mindbody depends on the minus of IT, to shine forever She.

Sapling's Apology

could it be that he is afraid,
you are the man in the woods
threatening with knife, tempting
to cut out his innocence for future use –
        in dying man's nightmare?

could it be that he is afraid,
you are the man in the woods
who froze his throat and filled his mouth
for nothing more than a release –
        of the tadpoles of Endorphine Creek?

could it be that he is angry,
we useless saplings were
just up the street, a rough-edged skipping stone
away from the clenched voice –
        of my big brother?

could it be that I I am angry,
for had I heard him
not even my tap root could have prevented me
from becoming the mighty predator
who would have left the bladed-prey –
        without a prayer?

ON~~UN~~BECOMING: Aesthetic Evolution of This Rising Ancestor

ON~~UN~~BECOMING: Aesthetic Evolution of This Rising Ancestor

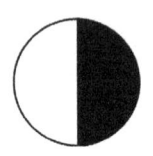

Chapter 6: gratitUde

∞

Symbiotic Light[H]er and nicotine
is the oddest trinity pair.

Vertebrae Rising

I know you well enough
to give thanks
for what allows me
to not know you.

My inflexible spine triggered
by the third entity unique to we
shields [y]our darkest potential's
release.

Over, Around, Under, and Through

her formerly-assembled myelin sheath
is so obviously woven tightly
with barbed wire, it is difficult
to escape the thistle-like tendrils
of her metallic mind.

the wire cutters of humility
keep pace, cutting through
all the shadowed bullshit
like a moonlit metronome.

as her imprisoned exorcism completes,
she discovers the portal, escapes
from all she is going
over, around, under, and through -

she rises.

her commitment to the crawl
consistent, the musketeers
know this better than she believes.

their faith in their faith in her,
the wire cutters of humility,
and moonlit metronome
rushes, pools, resonates
over, around, under, and through -

she rises up.

rehabilitation is not about the speed of her Light,
rather the community that exists
over, around, under, and through
her side of
her troubled
mind's line –

She is risen.

Daft Light

Yes, Teacher, I will remember the
Light in what we fear.

How could I forget?
The song played when the moon was full and
fireflies hovered over earth, lighthouses –
patiently resting on daft reservoir blades.

My eyes remember:
The song of Light wasn't heard in the eyes of dark sky,
when the smirk of the crescent synced with a
single, charmed winking star.

My second skin remembers:
The covert sliver of a pin\n\ing pupil of Mx. Moon.
During the period of eclipse where shame's arrow
unconsciously, and yet quite wittingly
stuck cleanly through the heart of it.

My soul now speaks;
I hope one day to meet you,
and yet never see you
again, madness
behind the moon.

Thank you, Teacher.
Now I can forget.

It's Poetic Justice Until We All Lose Our Eyes

My story
        is so nearly relevant,
        I forget and roll my eyes.
        Devil in savior's clothes
        Selects scared women,
        To satiate he's primal power – a peculiar brand of joy.

        (climax)

        his ego & impatient impulses
        blind him, his triangulated
        pitted fruit gather, with
        selfless, patient pistols resting
        at their Soldier Hips.
        Protests him out of town.

        climax

Our story
        Has a modern twist with
        An ancient form of NEVER FORGET:
        As in, forgive as if Our lives depend on it,
        because they does.

        (chance)

        If we are to distort the ideal of power,
        We must *choose* to call him Savior
        and wash our calloused feet
        as well as his. Disgusting
        for some, I see.

        chance

It is clear to me, the matriarch of
his chosen polygamy,
that the Collective Voice uniquely
hears this silence within this noise.
The humming humbling mumble

Perhaps there is no means to this end.
Perhaps the devil's clothes were a costume for him.
Perhaps he has yet to take it off since that glowing October day
when his mother bought it as a reward for keeping quiet.
His coveted, covert-emboldening
mass-produced, polyester Batman suit.

change

Faithing with My Tidal Power

Truth exists
in the inebriated scream
rising from the cave
man's soul.

I hear, most often,
A lonely, mournful howl and
Shame-inoculated raging whispers.

With a humble drop of my shoulder's chip,
nestled as the distant moon,
I realize the power this fraught
cycle brings to man's toxic stalagmite-
encrusted insides.

The mazed cave of secrets fills.
Toxic drink floods,
a sweet detoxifying tsunami for
the shadowed soul.

It is now time for me to go,
to camouflage against blue sky.
The sun is rising, and
it is Light's time.

I am still here, out in full,
even when in parts -
Faithing with my tidal powers.

Steadied by a universal knowing -
        intoxicating rays of pure sunlight
        invite the belly cave
        close enough to the edge of safety,
        relinquishing control to the imagination.

ON~~UN~~BECOMING: Aesthetic Evolution of This Rising Ancestor

Once a cave, now a star-lit pore
on the surface of man's already
beautiful, canvased skin.

Return to the Crooked Willow

When She is home
a little crooked and hanging
her wrapped roots exposed
She is planted here in front of you
to be;
        admired,
        climbed on,
        nested in.

If you long
to follow lines and tracks
reaching to the heavens
or the dirt, remember;
it is priceless – the not seeking with certainty, the up or down.

If her painted lines are home,
She is planted here for you.
{Your link to Her is beyond flesh, closer to blood.}

If you can forget yourself
in her map of circled rings
of yesterday's growth, remember;
each ring is a valid version of the truth.
{Valued reflections in algae covered toad ponds.}

If her version of truth soothes you,
She is planted here for you.

In your backyard,
wherever it may be,
She is with you.

In your heart, rooted
your home, growing –
in the forest of the west.

When your ashes need a lullaby,
promise to return to Her;
      cell to cell,
      lines to lines,
      map to map,
      truth to truth.

She will serve your nitrogen
to the saplings and the aged,
through me, the misunderstood
fungus of the forest floor.

Your birthplace, your buried place;
where the other woodland creatures don't question
your worth, like you did while on your walk.

Where you are greeted with circular, purposeful gratitude.

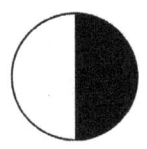

ON~~UN~~BECOMING: Aesthetic Evolution of This Rising Ancestor

ON~~UN~~BECOMING: Aesthetic Evolution of This Rising Ancestor

Chapter 7: exHail WITH the IN

∞

The tick tock of Time might just be
the sound of righteous Light.

Good, Then Extra

Today She was reminded how She clings to the past
Like an image of something they both loved
And yet, you've moved on
And yet, you didn't tell her
And then, She catches fire
Attempting, again, to lite
the very short and
water-soaked
~~wick~~. ~~tether~~. cord.

Rather than jumping over this moment
Pretending loss is an inevitability
Of set-them-free love
Of unconditional love
She lets go her control
and grieves.

Ugh. (sigh)

OUCH! (sound of heartbelly tearing)

"Is it over yet?" she asks me,

>a card-carrying member of a courageously-fragile, age-old club:
>The Immortalled-Portalled Wombs.

>I reply, "It never ends. It never begins."

***

I know why
His/Hers/Theirs
Does not precisely align with the inner me

From now on I want to be called a
Smooth-skinned fucking man with an
Unstandardizeable-portalled womb

"Is that too much to ask?" I ask

                                    "Blah blah blah,"
      "Blah blah blah,"
                                                                              "Blah blah
                                                                                        blah,"
                      "Blah blah blah,"

They speak.

     "   ," I reply

Malignant Phraseology Vol. 1: "You're the Crazy One"

I hung up the phone. I heard your eye's screaming whisper, catching those blinding-dark glimpses behind my recycled aluminum mask. How dare you question me with able-minded accounts.

Look away, over there, inside the you that voluntarily drank the unknowingly spiked Kool-Aid just yesterday.

Is that she okay? I know I am.

...

>Follow my right hand.
>In it is your Soul. Watch yourSelf rise
>and fall, and fall,
>and fall into the dirt.
>
>Again, focus on my correct hand.
>In it is the Truth. Watch yourTongue wonder
>and waver, and waver,
>and waver into the abyss.
>
>Now, now.
>No, no.
>Don't look at the deception of
>this left moment.
>
>Again, see my strong fisted hand.
>See it opening, releasing you,
>dropping you. Oh dear,
>don't break.
>
>Now, now.
>Yes, yes.
>Look right here.
>I will catch you, fragile one.

See? You do need help.

...

I can help. I am both the malignancy and the oncologist. I know best. I can treat you, and the disease that is you, like no other. The overtly, overly patient-patient that you learned to be. I caught the whiff of this deep-in-your-marrow disease early on. That stench of worthless antibodies, unable to fight off even the common cold shoulder.

Now, now. All you need is this slow chemical drip. My mind-numbing medicine will wipe out all that is good and, if you don't die from that, whatever is left will label you "survivor."

By this time I will have moved my practice somewhere more prestigious than you, perhaps even the White House. You can send your wax-embossed "thank you" note by post. I will smell you when it arrives because I have a strong sense of things. The memory of what you meant to me, will be with me, in my upgraded Situation Room.

Familiar, Familial Border

When do unattended-to childhood patterns
Turn away from shame and
Toward intentional tools of destruction
Requiring only a whispered demand to be
handed the bleeding hearts' supply.

They count on your sadness to
Fill their bottomless cup of gladness
And before you know it
You've been punched in the eye
Swallowing excuses,
like in generations of reels passed down.

Know, that is all a distraction,
While drain pipes are inserted
Behind your heart
Where the rainy day soul-juice pools.

When does "They don't know better"
Become "I'm no longer a consistent supply."

Upon my dreamland's synthetic reflection
We can all agree on the natural disaster of a wounded child
But once you're
      Self-aware enough to manipulate truth
      Seeded enough to sprout a beard
      Your pride speaks like you have grown a pair
Don't remain unattractive.

Turn that testosterone
On yourself
And fight your demons

Like the Earth's life depends on it
{because it actually does}
Until only humble, grateful, love is left.

Find your gifted silver lining
Your everything within your nothing
Like the rest of us.

No longer parade your prolonged adolescence
Like that other soldier's purple heart
It is an insult to the asylum seekers of this day
and crushes the potential they hold.

Our only supply left, to have faith in our faith
{Yes, resistance is a form of faith.}
You are no longer a childhood victim
You have chosen the plaque of 'shameless scoundrel'.

Imagine the energy harnessed
In transforming your self-indulgent scars
And taking your place
In the battlefield you know too well.

Become a righteous role model
To the alien children of today
Crossing your, only too
familiar, familial border.

Between what could be today's here
And long ago's hell.

plated projection

I hate him
like I hate ebola.

I hate the hims
like I hate the number
of not empty pews.

I hate them
like I hate the kind of
time passing that
births putrid toes
while arguing over
the truth of the frigid vortex.

I hate us
like I hate the blissful ignorance of
bees and lions
who could flatten us
if they would
wake the fuck up and show their superpower;
        a long vacation for the buzzing,
        a coordinated feeding for the
        palm-lengthed teeth of the
        purring beast.

I hate myself
like I hate the inability to alter
the direction the world spins.

ebola
time passing
blissful ignorance
the unchangeable direction of all things.

ON~~UN~~BECOMING: Aesthetic Evolution of This Rising Ancestor

hIm.
hIms.
them.
us.
purrIng prIde.
buzzIng swarm.
myself.

am I more IndIgnant or
more exhausted?

I guess,
what I actually hate,
Is numbed IndecIsIon.

forgIve that and
I have lIcked the plate
Clean.

              NOTE TO SELF:
      ALWAYS LEAVE A LiTTLE
HONEY AND CREAM ON YOUR PLATE,
AS YOUR DEMONSTRATiON OF FAiTH.

           THE BUZZiNG AND
          PURRiNG CREATURES
       ARE NOT AS HELPLESS
      AS WE ayes PROJECT.

ON~~UN~~BECOMING: Aesthetic Evolution of This Rising Ancestor

waking in the center of The Dark Triad

in grief, we rebel against oursouls
towards the Narcissist's obtuse angle.
we lite the gas stove, invite the dark to our Thanks-
giving table, offer Him a crown.
He accepts willingly, tempting the con
of dying on the rearward cross for this meager sin.

in our serotonin-rich slumber,
we integrate past and present, reorganize truths
as the myelin sheath of His unproven right triangle seals shut.
the agentic state of our cult-mind bakes
in the dry, desert sun.

numbed,
we adjust our eyes to the blindkindness,
open bolted doors -

The Dark Triad with a[d]version enters.

**

after the quenchstorming, we wake soaking in truth;
    we have become the axis of evil that knocked loose
    the Machiavellian marbles of our former Vice.
    his Psychopathy-packed patriot[ic] act[ion]
    picked at the scab of then's fresh grief, offering
    Us the slow drip of today's red threat scribed in yesterday's
    Milgram mani-
    Festo

    {when we rebel against our grief. we do not walk towards.}

NEVER FORGET:
planes collided, towers fell. surveillance rose
by the very pen of our POTUS's tender\Barr.

**

in a state of domestic dissonance, our learnt
Narcissistic flea-covered marbles
smother the floor. Intoxicated; we trip, stumble,
fall into our exhaustion.
blinders fall. this is not a threesome,
rather we are
master\bating
in the darkness, under the sheets,
in the oval rest-room, filled with our fecal matter
of projected stooled growth.

all the while our crowned Guest,
his Barr\tender[s], and our Master's Vice[s]
flash their matching badges
at the endless intersections within
The Institutionalized Dark Triad -
burning calories on the upthrust.

their now heavily-branded society is hungry,
again needs feeding.
we may nourish them or
their fearless-form of scarcity.
in not choosing our fa\te\ith
is sealed - be it in hell or heaven.
meager time on earth remains.

***

the meal is over.

the dessert tray is -given
Thanks-, but I no longer eat sweets
with a cherry on top.

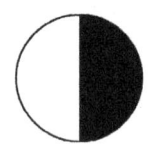

ON~~UN~~BECOMING: Aesthetic Evolution of This Rising Ancestor

ON~~UN~~BECOMING: Aesthetic Evolution of This Rising Ancestor

Chapter 8: AFTER THANKS is GIVEN

∞

Although important to you,
Hokis' Light recuses Herself
to the non-smoking section.

[s]PACING OF CONSTANTS

{The need to control is the masc of fear.}

Deaf thee tore me,
not of this room.

Letting the remaining
Constant, consonants go
       nts,
       clr,
       c.

Reminder within remains;
       note to self,
       clear,
       conscience.

...
Masc is the abbreviation for the traditional meaning of masculinity.

Altering the Mind of Gravity

Love cannot permeate the busy-brained heart, just
Ask the stretching-self-over-the-valley dendrite.
Muscle memories of
Icy, undertow moments from
Comrades and rivals, alike.
Time to decelerate, my small white elliptical
Axis holds my revolving leash, I twist to reach blue sky
Love-enabled lubricated sheath, now sets this synapse free.

...
Lamictal is a medication used to treat seizures as well as regulate extreme moods of those with complex trauma and bipolar disorder.

Preference Over Judgement

Self-love
Puppy love
First love
Unrequited love
Pining for first love, love
Pining for first love lost, love
Pining for the second love lost, love
Pining becomes love, love
I hear someone in every song, love
Addicted to love, love
Addicted to the novelty of falling into love, love

Promised love
Pay off for your dysfunctions, codependent love
Separated love
Divorced love
You cannot be who I need, projected anger, love
I cannot be who you need, projected shame, love
Trauma-inoculated fear of abandonment love
Trauma-inoculated I overshared, shameful and regretful, self-hate, and inch away from love, kind of love
Pathological altruism, codependent as fuck love

Turn towards each other love
Turn away from each other love
Turn against each other love

Letting go of any love but self-love, love
Forgiving, humble, deeply rooted in higher purpose love
Accepting you, just as you are, taking responsibility for myself love
Surrendering into my soul love

Love that never was, mind plays tricks, love
Love that never will be, star-struck and seductive tendril, love
The universe sent you to teach me something love

ON~~UN~~BECOMING: Aesthetic Evolution of This Rising Ancestor

Octopus momma,
starving to death, while staying with her eggs kind of love
I will carry you if you sting my predators,
crab and anemone kind of love
I trust you to not eat me if I clean your teeth,
eel and shrimp kind of love
You will travel far on my back if you eat my ticks,
parallel path, buffalo and bird kind of love
I can pick you out of a crowd of look-alikes, penguin love
I will wait by the shore each year, to dance, mate and
nest with only you, Albatros kind of love
A pride of lions, communal love
I will wake you up, play with you, protect you,
and accept your scraps, grateful dog and depressed human kind of
love.

Doing the dishes love
Making time love
Remembering details love
Friendship love
Holding space with open ears love

All of you is exactly what I love, love
I cannot handle all of you, compassionately stated, love
I cannot handle all of you, shamefully stated, projected anger, love

Orgy, what finger in what hole is irrelevant kind of love
Medicinal flesh kind of love
I adore the shape of my skin kind of self-love
My body is but a vessel for love, love
Consensual, controlling sex kind of love
Powered sex, collapsing into vulnerability kind of love
Kissing only love
No kissing allowed love
When we kiss, fall into myself and be fully present with your fall kind
of love

Kill for you love
Depart so you can love, love

Letting you go love
Born of you love
Born of other love

Sibling love
Favorite sibling love
Rather not have you as a sibling love

Parental contract love
Parent is my person love

Hold the hand of the passing love
I release you, love
Grieving love
Pain sparked growth self-love, love

Falling into love, love
Rising into love, love

It's all rising because of love,

Love.

Synapse Surfing

When I close my eyes and reach for the wall,
when my presence disappears

                                                                {this is now}
                (this is now)

    {this is now}
                        (this is now)

know I am strong –
feet solid on my board
synapse surfing
eye to eye
with the Great
White inside.

You may think I touch to please –
to play\for[e] me, for you.

        (I forgive you for this privileged thought, only if you commit to
        its demise. Otherwise the sticky white of greatness will spawn
        in us both – unmistakably alive.)

I memorize your body–
curves, fuzzies
smile lines

sound buttons, dimples
angles of bones
strength of boner.

Uwinding my synapse
to paint a new memory
a now memory
with the HUmility I pine for.

A one-at-a-time memory made with
my present –
my standard HUman.

Sleeping Beauty

Love is a word I leave for myself.
I am grateful for you,
my mirror honored for the reflection you trust enough to share.

Spider sense tingles,
I might lean in for a kiss, today
(perhaps tomorrow).

Present presence,
Perhaps a red delicious lover
(but not a core).

Care for my darkness, even in the Light
(with no bite)
you could be awarded the single jeweled crown,
though, I have no urgency to lift the glass exhibit case.

If I don't follow the progression,
      If I dishonor the quivering,
      closed-throat moments
      heart-racing moments
      wishing it were over whispers.

      Incumming! Incoming!
      Seeds of arsenic
      Taste the darkness
      I sank my teeth in too deep.

      Awake with anger
                cues of havoc
                              in my honored private place.

It's time to rest.
Don't feed the evil Queen.
(I am sorry she poisoned you.)

It's time to rest, forget all we've seen.

ON~~UN~~BECOMING: Aesthetic Evolution of This Rising Ancestor

ON~~UN~~BECOMING: Aesthetic Evolution of This Rising Ancestor

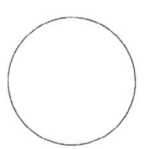

ON~~UN~~BECOMING: Aesthetic Evolution of This Rising Ancestor

Chapter 9: ACHEKNOWLEDGEments

∞

The gas-free torch, now lit,
shines from that moon
on the other side.

Ancestral Rise

Never really bought into
"falling" into love. I believe in the
Mystical "rising" into love.
The fairy dust of
ancestral work.

The initial dopamine seed hooks into dirt.
The slow growth of oxytocin filled fibrous roots.
Beauty grows.
The rising of oxygen.
The neverending kiss of
Heaven and Earth, breathes,
as we unfold all of who we are in the
Presence of another -
Commitment.

Accepted fully, not enmeshed.
Just as the
weeping willow
admires the
sequoia.

From here the tap root
grabs hold
deep, grounded.

Engages the
forest ecosystem.
Surrenders to the
laws of nature.

Each species
reflecting permission to the other.

Canopies reach into the sky,
to see the world from above,
to find the blue above
earthly-story-clouds.

Eventually, each reaches
the heavens or, perhaps,
distant galaxies.

The fairy dust falls, again.
The work of the ancestors continues.

Arrow Through That Universal Moon

She is always looking for signs
For tells
Of the inevitable
      Pull back
      Run away
      Emotional departure

Convinced
There is no truth
Everything is temporary
Lies are no surprise
Life misspeaks to her
all the time

She wonders
{but i know.}
If She keeps this up,
Death will collect her for
A perpetual broken heart,
Blindness and laryngitis

It started with her first cry
Arrow straight through
Leaving her howling
Calling out to her Mayrig
Under that universal moon

Perpetual pining
Uncomfortable comfort
Is all the love
She knows to know

She now pleads ignorance
Pretends the moon is puncture-less
Falls into the salty Black Sea

Buoyant in this ancestral tide pool
Her eyes wide open
Howl remains, voice intact

She floats.
So much surface tension
In this ancient holy water
She pretends to trust
If life lies, She will too
For a little while

To herself, She whispers
"It is going to be just fine"

{I say She is right,
                                        I think.}

...

Mayrig *n. /mā/rig/* The Armenian word for "mother."

ON~~UN~~BECOMING: Aesthetic Evolution of This Rising Ancestor

Leader of the Free World

In the parlor,
She decides to finally take out
the baby-skin smooth walnut carpenter box.
It was gifted to her by Father Time two years ago.
A month before he boarded the train home.

Inside:
pink laced baby shoes,
a single jeweled crown, and
a plaque which reads:
'Leader of the Free World'.

She looks back up at
That Universal Moon,
to offer her a prideful grin.

They return the sentiment.

Hokis, they whisper, *may you rise in peace.*

ON~~UN~~BECOMING: Aesthetic Evolution of This Rising Ancestor

ON~~UN~~BECOMING: Aesthetic Evolution of This Rising Ancestor

In Summary
∞

It was one year after my father died. I was walking my aged miniature beagle on the most perfect of summer days: bright sun, cool breeze, with one small cloud looking over things. Then, there he was. The younger man with a full beard. The torch bearer with charming eyes and half-cocked smile walked past – our eyes locking for a whiff of a second. A moment later, a return glance. Lighting up the life in me that had been laid to rest with Dad. I found myself wondering who he was, where he was, and if I would see him again. It was exactly what this grieving daughter, this wife of an exhausted marriage, this near empty-nester wanted. It was the last thing she needed. Her wounds so deep, she was unsteady, unrooted, unlookingforwardtoeverything.

The second point of contact came. One afternoon at the public library I turned a corner and fate landed him right in front of me. We said hello, exchanged some playful words. This scene would repeat often. Within weeks he would be at my doorstep asking to borrow a needle and thread to patch a hole in his jeans. It was an hour of conversation, an hour of assessment. Looking back, I could say – I do say – I knew all along what he was up to. I say this so I can live with myself, but I don't know if it is true.

The self-help books call him "gaslighter." Today is Tuesday, so I call him "asshole" for wearing my microexpressions to embody me, to learn my wounds and weaknesses, then slice right through me. Today is Wednesday, so I call him "fucker" for shining his dusk through the cracks of my very own #MeToo. Today is Thursday, so I now call him "my suicide note," which is shorthand for Friday's "I willingly welcomed his dirty, burning, diesel-fueled torch into my home," or Saturday's "I have lost all hope in life and death as it was and forever will be."

Sundays are different, as they are meant to be. Typically, I recall his carefully curated notes shared through *Spotify*, his symphonic forms of orchestrated courtship swoon. I dive back into my "Tunnel I am Going Through" playlist. *This* summer's blue sky is cloudless as I walk my German Shepherd as Xavier Rudd, Fiona Apple, and John Prine play. Their lyrics of mixed meanings remind me of this mind of mine, this orphaned self's half-baked cult-mind that once begged all the hims to make it up for me.

On these evenings, my head shakes in disbelief, my breath roots me to the earth, and my hand waves to last week. I turn my senses towards the Moon - basking in our forgivenesses and tuning my ears to starlight's sounds. The echoes of astral infinity assure this rising ancestor - *trust, choose, be.*

ON~~UN~~BECOMING: Aesthetic Evolution of This Rising Ancestor

ONUNBECOMING: Aesthetic Evolution of This Rising Ancestor

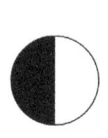

Glossary

∞

Aesthetic Evolution: A theory of evolutionary psychology in which the aesthetic preferences of a species have evolved to enhance their survival.

Mount Ararat: The "holy mountain" of the Armenian people, widely accepted in Christianity as the resting place of Noah's Ark. In the aftermath of the Armenian Genocide of 1915, Ararat came to represent the destruction of the native Armenian population of eastern Turkey in the national consciousness of Armenians.

Vulgata: The original Latin version of the Bible used by the Roman Catholic Church beginning in the 14th century.

Epigenetic: An additional genetic layer to our DNA sequence which influences which genes are expressed. The epigenome is influenced by environmental factors, inspiring research on inherited trauma.

Dark triad: The dark triad comprises the personality traits of narcissism, Machiavellianism, and psychopathy. They are called "dark" because of their evil qualities.

Narcissistic Personality Disorder (NPD): A mental disorder in which a person has an inflated sense of self-importance, a deep need for excessive attention and admiration, troubled relationships, and a lack of empathy for others. Although they appear extremely confident, a person with NPD has a fragile self-esteem - unable to take the slightest criticism.

Psychopathy: A mental disorder in which a person shows amoral and antisocial behavior, shows a lack of ability to love or establish meaningful personal relationships, and expresses extreme egocentricity.

Machiavellianism: A mental disorder in which a person is more likely to deceive and manipulate others for personal gain, often breaking ethical lines and utilizing legal loopholes to do so. They can have empathy if the person's diagnosis does not also include other antisocial disorders.

Narcissistic Fleas: Patterns of behaviors and habits a person adopted when being raised by a parent with narcissistic traits or narcissistic personality disorder. A person with narcissistic fleas can unlearn these patterns of behavior.

The Patriot Act: In the weeks after the September 11 (2001) attacks, Congress passed the "USA/Patriot Act." This was a revision of the nation's surveillance laws that allowed warrantless electronic data collection on its citizens, while also reducing judicial oversight, accountability, and the ability to challenge government searches in court. The current Attorney General, William Barr, designed this surveillance system.

UMF: In the days after the September 11 (2001) attacks, a legal document was drafted, and President George Bush signed it into law. This is known as Authorization for Use of Military Force (AUMF), which allowed the president to bypass congressional war powers to fight the "war on terror." The AUMF language allowed for the Guantanamo Bay detention camp, drone strikes, and the 2010 Patriot Act revisions. Examples of document's wording include "all necessary and appropriate force," "against those nations, organizations, or persons," and "in order to prevent."

Hokis *n.* /hō/kēs/ Armenian for "my soul" or "my beloved."

ON~~UN~~BECOMING: Aesthetic Evolution of This Rising Ancestor

∞

Thank you to the following publications where many of these works first appeared: Ayaskala Online Journal, Caustic Frolic, Cloud Women's Quarterly Journal, For Women Who Roar, Headline Poetry & Press, Indie Blu(e), Laurels & Bells, littledeath, Nymphs Publishing, Paragon Press, Stentorian Bitch, Tiny Seed Literary Journal, and Truly U.

Made in the USA
Monee, IL
14 November 2020